gardens by design ❧ THE NATIONAL TRUST

wild flowers

GRAHAM MURPHY

To His Holiness the XIV Dalai Lama

First published in 2004 by
National Trust Enterprises Ltd
36 Queen Anne's Gate, London SW1H 9AS

www.nationaltrust.org.uk

Cataloguing in Publication Data is available from the British
Library

ISBN 0 7078 0373 X

Designed by Barbara Mercer
Colour origination by Digital Imaging Ltd
Printed and bound in Hong Kong by Printing Express Ltd

Front cover: Corn Poppy (*Papaver rhoeas*).

Back cover: Herb Robert.

Page 1: A close-up of Corn Poppy petals.

Page 2: Meadow wild flowers at Castle Eden-Dene, Horden.

Contents

Introduction

Wild flowers bring to many of us remembrance of a lost world of childhood enchantment, of woodland, river and lush fields of flowery hay somewhat rare in real countryside. Names we once read in Kenneth Grahame's *The Wind in the Willows* – Loosestrife, Meadowsweet, Willowherb and Dog-rose – we perhaps think of no more. Although there is seldom a summer's day when we do not see Willowherb on waste ground or in a garden.

To re-awaken an affection for these flowers or perhaps to discover them for the first time, we do not need to be proficient in botany, herbalism, ecology, or even gardening. The slightest knowledge can yield immediate happiness. To notice one previously unfamiliar wild flower on the verge of a motorway when the traffic has ground to a halt is to take the mind away from exhausting anxieties and, for a few seconds at least, to know what it is to be at peace.

We are accustomed to thinking of wild flowers as plants with a long history. Some of them have been evolving on earth in forms we might now recognise for tens of millions of years. Others, like the blue Cornflower, have come to be associated with the period between 7,500 and 5,500 years ago, when cereal farming began, as traces of pollen have been discovered in pre-Neolithic remains. The term 'archeophyte' is used of species such as these, the origins of which are obscure but which are thought to be associated with human activity from ancient times.

The historic importance of wild flowers in relation to farming and sometimes as a food source, or as the material of medicines and natural dyes, is well known. What is more often underestimated is the part wild flowers play, in every age, in creative thinking. We are perhaps somewhat jaundiced in this respect, as we so often see them on all kinds

(*Above*): Dog Violet flower.

(*Opposite*): Bluebells in Frank's Wood, Leith Hill, Surrey.

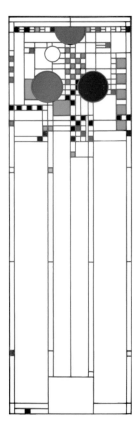

Playhouse, Illinois, 1912, by Frank Lloyd Wright: 'formal elements ... held well together in scale and character ... from some plant form that has appealed to me' – in this instance three flowerheads amid upper stem foliage, a basal leaf lower left.

of products, from bottles of shampoo to placemats. Clothes, rugs and furnishings are replete with images of stylised wild flowers, not always looking as pleasing as they might. Yet the leader of the Arts and Crafts movement, William Morris (1834–96), grew both wild and cultivated flowers in his garden, which he used as models for some of the most appealing designs ever to be printed on fabrics. The gorgeous patterns of Islamic art on the ceramics of Iznik in sixteenth-century Turkey were similarly inspired by the local flora (*see opposite*). Although the names of the glaze decorators have not survived, we can identify the work of particular crafts families by their use of a motif, such as trails of Wild Hyacinth.

Similarly, Willowherb, Gorse, Violet, Lady's Smock, Thrift and Snake's Head Fritillary were all drawn with consummate skill by the architect Charles Rennie Mackintosh (1868–1928). Elegant, though less clearly identifiable flower-motifs were used by him for the design and decoration of buildings and furniture. In North America, Frank Lloyd Wright (1869–1959) took this abstraction a stage further. From his own black and white photographs, he reproduced wildflower shapes and proportions in his buildings. We may no longer perceive a particular species in the design but are made aware that from somewhere a structure of considerable grace and charm has materialised.

Given the importance of these plants for so many areas of human activity, not forgetting fine art, literature and botany, it seems remarkable that the recognition of common species is not widely taught. In one of his regular gardening columns in *The Financial Times* (7 June 2003), the Oxford classicist, Robin Lane Fox, complained that 'in the past thirty years, I have been lucky enough to teach the nation's brightest, but none of them had a clue what a primrose looks like'.

We might therefore understand a lack of sensitivity to the countryside, where the new owners of farmhouses and converted barns turn once colourful trackside banks and

Stonepaste dish from Ottoman Turkey (Iznik, *c.*1545–50) with underglaze painting featuring naturalistic flower designs of trailing hyacinths.

verges into green lawns, in case they look untidy. Primrose might survive such an improvement for a while, but not Red Campion or Common Knapweed.

Our Victorian and Edwardian ancestors were more aware of wild flowers. The high public profile of plant-collectors such as Sir Joseph Banks, and the friction between theology and science raised by Charles Darwin, aroused such an interest in botany that the subject was considered essential to a good general knowledge. But, more importantly perhaps, the art critic and writer, John Ruskin, attracted the allegiance of undergraduates and captured the sympathy of educated women. He more than anyone directed their minds to the study of wild flowers, almost in preference to an interest in formal gardening.

We may wonder what encourages a child today to become an enthusiastic amateur botanist or an eco-warrior defending a bluebell wood. The passions aroused by a deprivation of what the mystic poet, Thomas Traherne (c.1636–74), identified as the common human need 'to enjoy the world aright', can sometimes produce a powerful reaction. When a pond by a Cheshire footpath where I walk was filled with rubble (as part of a grant-aided scheme to improve field drainage), it felt to me as if someone had burned down my local library. I had barely begun to notice Yellow Flag iris and dragonflies before this priceless amenity was abolished.

The public at large has given an answer to this loss of wildlife culture. Homeowners have turned to building ponds and sowing packets of cornfield annuals. But the danger is that conservation then becomes only a memorial activity consigned to gardens and museum landscapes.

Sixty years ago British naturalists saw little need to be anxious about the prevalence of common wild flowers in the countryside. One had just to take a bus ride to the edge of a town or city to find fields, woods and riverbanks full of them. Their main concern was for rare plants in remote places, in habitats they wished to designate as nature reserves. These sites were also, fortunately, in areas of renowned natural beauty, for the preservation of which the public would readily subscribe to organisations like the National Trust. The Lizard in Cornwall is a fine example, and Wicken Fen in Cambridgeshire another, the first few acres of which were acquired by the Trust in 1899.

Government subsidies for farming and the growth of towns and cities caused a massive loss of Britain's wild flowers in the second half of the twentieth century. Common species were in one way or another eradicated from cornfields and most meadows. Half of our

Wild daffodils mixed with other flowers at the side of a path at the Weir, Swainshill, Herefordshire.

11

nation's heaths, three-quarters of downland sheep-walks and half of the lowland fens and mires were destroyed by a combination of urbanisation and agricultural land improvements. About half of all ancient deciduous woods were felled.

In the sort of project which now seldom takes place in a science curriculum, a class of first-year secondary schoolchildren at the County High School, Arnold, on the northern edge of Nottingham, was asked to make books of pressed flowers during the spring and summer school holidays of 1962. With the aid of an *Observer's Book of British Wild Flowers*, twelve-year-old Sandra Marsh collected and identified ninety-two species from around

Wild flowers growing round a tree trunk create a romantic and evocative sight in spring.

the villages of Lambley, Woodborough and Epperstone. With landowners' permissions, a repetition of her homework today would yield useful comparative data, particularly in respect of the loss of wild flowers due to persistent crop spraying. Schoolchildren's records of that period and earlier, where they still exist, are a valuable resource for assessing the impact of intensive farming.

One manifestation of ecological catastrophe in the heartlands of North America was only narrowly averted here in Britain. In the 1950s, commercial interests had tried to persuade the highway authorities to adopt the regular spraying of modern herbicides on roadside verges. This proposal was voted

Old Man's Beard or Traveller's Joy (Wild Clematis) seedhead in January.

down under pressure from naturalists, who expressed their horror at such a scheme through a government agency, the Nature Conservancy Council, now renamed English Nature. On pasture and arable land, however, the use of chemicals was unrestrained. Wildflower colonies which had existed for centuries were steadily, year by year, depleted. Not until the 1990s was chemical destruction effectively abated by a combination of 'set-aside', the widening of field margins and on some farms the introduction of purely organic methods of cultivation.

One voluntary organisation had been opposing all manner of threats to the beauty of ordinary country since its foundation, by an elite social group, in 1926. However, so overwhelming was the effect of intensive agriculture – the loss of hedgerows and other concomitant degradations on farmland – that the Campaign to Protect Rural England was moved to re-appraise its effectiveness and seek wider membership. Organisations of more recent origin have entered the arena, to help protect and re-establish wild flowers wherever there are open spaces capable of better management and restoration: the Wildlife Trusts, Plantlife, Common Ground and Landlife are among these. In addition, there has been a steady influence on government policies from scientific bodies such as the Botanical Society of the British Isles, and the British Ecological Society, founded in 1913.

Science of a kind which values wild flowers can be traced back to the ancient Greeks. Theophrastus (c.372–286BC), a pupil and friend of both Plato and Aristotle, is generally acknowledged to have been the founding father of botany. Describing the structure and location of herbs and wild flowers, he enabled them to be more easily identified. This was of primary importance to early physicians such as Dioscorides, whose first-century *De Materia Medica* was a source of herbal knowledge throughout the Middle Ages.

In ancient India, plants useful as medicines were likewise recorded and classified, according to seven forms of their structure. Knowledge of herbs and wild flowers was also an essential part of Arabian pharmacology. In China the scholar Li Shih-Chen compiled *The Great Pharmocopoeia* (1596). Drawing on the works of previous physicians, the volume is reputed to describe a thousand plants, a thousand animals and eight-thousand medicinal prescriptions.

Even before the scheme of Latin names for all animals and plants devised by the Swedish botanist, Carl Linnaeus (1707–78), by the sixteenth century the invention of printing had brought about a more systematic approach to the recognition and naming of wild flowers in Western Europe. New herbals and books of botany, building on classical texts, increased the list of known plants, setting them in better order. Names and descriptions were sometimes accompanied by wood-block-printed pictures of the flowers growing in typical association with other wild plants and grasses. As descriptions of all types of living organisms proliferated, a broader interest in the world of nature was defined by the term, 'Natural History'.

In the University of Cambridge, for most of the second half of the seventeenth century Natural History was taught by John Ray (1627–1705). His ambitious aim was to produce a systematic description of the entire organic world – all its plants, animals, insects, birds and fishes – in an endeavour to explain the seemingly miraculous way in which God's creation fitted together and worked. It is plain to see in Ray's work and that of his disciple Gilbert White (1720–93) an anticipation of what most people think of today as 'ecology'. This modern word was coined and first used by German and Danish naturalists to describe the distribution of plants in relation to various conditions of soil, light, humidity, exposure to weather and the effects of other living organisms. 'Ecology', however, soon gained such a broad meaning that it has sometimes been daubed 'the scientific cloak for what had long been known as natural history'.

There is no better introduction to Natural History than the work of Gilbert White, although he is now regarded as of merely arcane interest by many academics. His *Natural History of Selborne* (1789) gives us a vivid picture of a Hampshire country parish through the eyes of a man with an enormous respect for nature and the pure dispassion of a scientist. The book was little read until a

The Long Lythe at Selborne, Hampshire, with Cuckoo flowers in the foreground.

magazine article in 1830 awakened public interest. Since then, there has seldom been a year in which it has not been republished. By that time also, migration into the industrialised towns and cities had caused White's pristine vision of the English countryside to be, for an increasing number of people, a world no longer theirs to enjoy each day.

As Gilbert White's *Natural History of Selborne* reminded its readers what it was about the countryside they missed, the many amateur enthusiasts, desirous of specifically botanical knowledge, were catered for by a range of detailed manuals. On Sunday afternoons and the new Bank holidays, a favourite past-time was to wander country lanes and common lands carrying one of the many reprints of Charles Babington's *British Botany*, George Bentham's *Handbook of British Flora*, or the Reverend C.A. Johns's *Flowers of the Field*. For general reading, Ruskin strongly recommended the quaintly entitled *Ladies' Botany* (1837–8) by John Lindley, a genius of horticulture and Professor of Botany in the University of London. The finest publication of all was John Sowerby's *Concise Encyclopedia of Wild Flowers* (1860), described as 'a volume of reference for the field botanist ... or the summer

rambler'. It contained concise and detailed prints of all the wild flowers, every one of which was hand-coloured.

Even in children's books, Latin names began to appear alongside the better-known common names of wild flowers. A case in point is M.M. Rankin's *A First Book of Wild Flowers* (1909), the earliest to have a colour-printed illustration for each of the more than 90 featured flowers. With every passing year of the First World War, there appeared a new edition of this book. From those that have survived, it is evident that as well as being offered as Sunday School prizes, they were also used as parting gifts by fathers and uncles before their departure to the trenches.

Throughout the Victorian and Edwardian eras, wild flowers had become immensely popular in the minds of townsfolk, for their association with romantic notions of countryside. Both in imagination and practice, the ideal cottage-style garden was a place where cultivated and wild flowers co-existed. Often of necessity wild flowers were grown, because they could be collected from woods and hedge-banks at no expense to the gardener, when there was insufficient income to spend on plants from a nursery. Primroses would be planted in the shade of a garden tree, seed of Columbine cast between shrubs and hardy perennials. Foxglove, Common Comfrey and Sweet Cicely had their places among the herbs. In the 1880s, a botanist in the West Riding of Yorkshire complained that Bloody Cranesbill was being decimated in the wild, 'being so handsome' to gardeners.

Although the law now protects common wild flowers from the predations of gardeners, there is much to be said for lawfully continuing the tradition of wildflower planting. The garden writer, William Robinson, made wild gardens

(*Opposite*): Wild flowers, including Red Campion, Alkonet, Bluebell and Herb Robert.

(*Below*): A single Herb Robert flower.

fashionable for his wealthy clients from about 1870 onwards, but he was concerned with appearances and not ecology. The present revival of interest in the subject stems from a concern to encourage biodiversity, attracting small birds, moths and butterflies, bees, frogs and even snails.

The building of ponds, the planting of beech hedges and native trees, the preference for unpainted natural materials and low dry stone walls – all make a garden more attractive for wildlife. These features provide an excellent structure for an informal style of garden, planted with colonies of wild flowers in their appropriate locations. Despite the current fashion for decks and gravel, a lawn is still potentially one of the most beautiful features in an average garden, but only if it is not dosed with 'weed and feed' and fine-cut as if for a game of bowls. Children ought not to be denied their place to make daisy chains, test for Butter-glow, taste Clover-honey, pick violets and watch bees dancing with Self-Heal. The Sikh guru, Har Rai (1630–61), was so horrified when the flap of his coat once decapitated a flower that, ever after, he held it folded on his arm. Likewise, we need to hold the mower-blades a little above the wild plants and when they bloom, towards the end of May, suspend cutting for three weeks or so. Given the entertainment these low-growing flowers offer us, it is surprising they are not value-added components of lawn turf.

Even a modest wildflower meadow is possible as part of a garden, if the topsoil can be removed and seeded according to the type of subsoil. Seed mixtures incorporating Yellow Rattle, which is semi-parasitic on grasses, can sometimes maintain the vital balance required to keep the meadow full of flowers and seed-heads prior to the hay harvest.

No flowers blend more sweetly together than those of old hay meadows. Looking down the slopes of Dovedale in Derbyshire, a survivor of the English Civil War once observed a boy and a girl playing amid the 'Lilies and Lady's-smocks … Culverkeyes and

Cowslips'. He called to mind an ancient Greek myth of a field in which hunting-packs were caused 'to fall off, and to lose their hottest scent'. The reason for the dogs' distraction was that 'these, and many other field flowers so perfumed the air'.

The fields of Dovedale thus described by Izaak Walton in *The Compleat Angler* (1653) miraculously escaped all land improvements of succeeding centuries and happily survive in the care of the National Trust to the present day. In town gardens and countryside, in parks and beside motorways, our present opportunity is to make landscape ever more hospitable towards wild flowers, and to design with a care for nature's own history of beauty in our land.

Wild orchids and buttercups in the orchard at Glendurgan Garden near Falmouth, Cornwall.

family: **lily**
situation: **semi-shade**
colour: **blue**
height: **25–30cm (10–12in)**
in flower: **April–June**
ground: **well-drained, acid**
cultivation: **bulb**

Bluebell

Hyacinthoides non-scripta

The Bluebell is a form of hyacinth. Its likeness to potted hyacinths in the supermarket best seen in the shape of the small flower-bells. Both the wild and cultivated flowers share an ancient Greek story, alluded to in Virgil's *Eclogues* (iii, 106). The first of their type allegedly sprang up from the blood of a dying prince called Hyacinth. His death so mortified the god Apollo that in grief he inscribed the leaves of these archetypal plants with the letters AI ('alas').

In what we think of as real history, there came to the notice of botanists in the Roman world a limp-looking flower, confined solely to Britain, at the northern limits of the Empire. This plant bore every characteristic of the archetype, save for the god's inscription. So they named it *Hyacinthoides non-scripta*.

Apart from citations by the more adventurous herbalists – as a remedy against leprosy, tuberculosis and spider-bites – the drooping and poisonous British bluebells subsequently received scant appreciation. Only in the nineteenth century did the sight of masses of these flowers, in woods and bracken, awaken the interest of the Romantic poets. Gerard Manley Hopkins later wrote of 'light beating up from so many glassy heads … like water', 'wash wet like lakes' (*Journal*, 11 May 1873).

A lighter-coloured Spanish Bluebell (*Hyacinthoides hispanica*) has since hybridised with our native flowers, causing some loss of the real lake-like magic, especially in woods not far isolated from gardens. The British bluebells can be distinguished from interlopers by their narrower leaves (7–15mm). A native flower also has a more drooping stem with smaller, nodding flower-bells, each with little petals that roll back onto the slim flower tube. Inside, the pollen on the stamens is cream in colour, never blue, and a cinnamic alcohol gives to the flower a spicy balsam-like scent.

Growing Bluebell flowers from seeds takes several years. However, the bulbs are now widely available. They propagate well beneath hedges and trees, feeding on the fungi of rotting leaves. Kept away from strong sunlight, the flowers will retain their mystical darkness.

Close-up showing the nodding flower-bells with petals rolling back onto the slim flower tube.

Bogbean
Manyanthes trifoliate

By common consent one of the very prettiest flowers of our land ... nevertheless, seems long in coming to its own with the generality of plant lovers.

Wild Flowers as they Grow, 1911

The botanist Clarke Nuttall's comment still holds true. This flower suffers from a dull name and the loss of places where it used to grow: shallow ponds, bogs and fens. My own knowledge of Bogbean comes from having built the pond in which I first made its acquaintance. It has thick, creeping roots that push their way over the mud 'like worms crawling'. Plants may be grown from seed pressed into the wet soil in spring, or propagated in spring and summer by division of the rhizome. A pond or bog garden that does not have this elegant perennial is lacking a treasure.

The flower buds of Bogbean are a bright rose-pink and when fully open look like white stars. However, they have a charming feature which has been described as freakish and there is nothing quite like it in any other British wild flower. 'Each petal is fringed with delicate white threads which give the flowers the beauty of frost crystals' (Stevens, 1987).

The great Linnaeus (see p.14), at work on his monumental study of the plants of Lapland, noticed that the locals used roots of Bogbean powdered, to bulk up the meal in their bread. The resulting loaves contained lots of nutritious starch but tasted bitter. The trifoliate leaves, likewise bitter, were at one time used in infusions for the alleviation of scurvy and rheumatism. The Dutch physician Hermann Boerhaave (1668–1738) – an extremely rich man by dint of his international clientele – claimed to have cured himself of gout by drinking Bogbean tea made with whey. But be warned, only a skilled herbalist should dry and measure compound of the leaves, as they can easily deteriorate.

family: **rose**

situation: **sun**

colour: **white**

height: **60cm (24in)**

in flower: **May–July**

ground: **well-drained**

cultivation: **plant**

Burnet Rose

Rosa pimpinellifolia

Of all wild roses – even more so than the Sweet Briar – the Burnet Rose is the most sweetly scented, a mixture of jasmine and honey. The shrub is low-growing, forming thickets by means of suckers. The dark stems are covered 'with fine bristly hairs and sharp prickles', and the small leaves are of seven to nine tiny, rounded leaflets, with finely serrated margins. In autumn, the hips are maroon to black, like large blackcurrants, the leaves then turn to 'brown and plum, with here and there a yellow leaf to add sparkle' (McMurtrie, 1998). Although it grows extensively on the west coast of Scotland and Ireland, the Burnet Rose is somewhat scarce in England. In Wales, it is to be found mainly on the sand dunes of the Pembrokeshire coast – the reason why it was chosen as the emblem of the See of St David.

Growing from seed, there is a high failure rate, even when the seed is properly over-wintered in moist compost for a year or two. Rooted suckers also seem not to take, and so a plant from an 'old rose' nursery, raised by an expert, is the solution. Scots Roses in general are a fascinating subject and sometimes a specialist nursery will have one or more of the cultivated varieties from this wildling. By far the most well known is the repeat-flowering 'Stanwell Perpetual'. Another to be greatly desired is 'Falkland' – pale-pink, semi-double, greyish-green foliage and somewhat rare.

I first noticed the lovely creamy-white flowers of Burnet Rose in the wild at Dunure in Ayrshire, where the flora is in such abundance that the entire shoreline – cliff, sand and rock – is like the setting of a fable, with the little castle and harbour at its centre. The fecundity of such landscape has been accurately captured by the Scottish School of painters, led by William McTaggart (1835–1910). They produced for a popular market works which were, until fairly recently, passed over for their sentimentality: children amid Scottish wild flowers, with sometimes heather or Burnet Roses, and in the background a summer sky and a gently restless sea.

family: **buttercup**
situation: **sun & semi-shade**
colour: **blue**
height: **30–90cm (12–35in)**
in flower: **May–July**
ground: **dry or slightly moist**
cultivation: **seed**

Columbine

Aquilegia vulgaris

Of all the varieties of Columbine, sadly, the wild flower has no scent. This lack of fragrance, however, is compensated for by its alluring colour, described by the Northamptonshire poet, John Clare, as 'stone-blew or deep night brown'. The flower's curvaceous shape is so unusual that Columbine was once a by-word for flattery. The Elizabethan poet Edmund Spenser sweetly opined that his wife's neck was 'like unto a bunch of cullambynes'. The flower is generally likened to the elegance of birds: the botanical name suggests an eagle (*aquila*), the common name is derived from the latin *columba*, meaning a dove. It requires little imagination to see that the five nectaries in the drooping flower head resemble dove-like creatures in a circle, as if in conference.

Limestone woods are the natural home of wild Columbine. When cheap railway travel made the villages of Devon more accessible to holidaymakers, many of our great-grandparents walked the country lanes and brought seed of this wild flower back to the city. The dark-coloured and hybridised descendants still appear in backyards and old gardens. A somewhat dry, fertile and slightly alkaline soil most favours Columbine and the flower looks particularly delightful in dappled shade. The seed needs to be sown in spring or early autumn; for companion planting use Martagon Lily and hardy cyclamen. To raise early flowers in the same location sow seeds of Violet, Wood Anemone and Woodruff.

The herbalist Nicholas Culpeper (1616–54) assigned Columbine to the influence of Venus. He went on to observe that 'the seed taken in wine causeth a speedy delivery of women in childbirth'. Hardly surprising – an infant conceived in love might well want to escape the influence of a plant which is in all parts somewhat poisonous.

family: **borage**

situation: **sun & part-shade**

colour: **creamy-white/blue**

height: **30–120cm (12–47in)**

in flower: **May–July**

ground: **moist**

cultivation: **root section**

Common Comfrey

Symphytum officinale

No garden should be without this versatile plant, beautifully soft in its appearance and of great practical value. The flowers are tubular, borne in clusters in a springing curve, like glimpses of a swinging bell. The leaves are oval and hairy, up to 25cm (10in) long at ground level and smaller the nearer they are to the top of the stem.

The English name seems to be from *confervere*, the latin verb for 'to grow together'. All parts of the plant have a reputation for healing cuts and fractures. Grating the roots produces a jelly-like paste which can be applied to lesions, or plastered over a fracture to reduce the swelling. Coalminers knew Common Comfrey for its ability to soothe 'beet knee', likewise abrasions and bruising to the elbows. An infusion of the leaves in warm water gives relief to sprained wrists and ankles. Not surprisingly, this plant often goes by the name of 'Knitbone'.

In the wild, Common Comfrey grows by rivers and in ditches. Its place in the garden therefore needs to be somewhat damp, but where the spreading of its roots can be contained. Starting the plant from seed is slow and erratic; the simplest method of propagation is to break off a section of root and transplant it.

The original apothecary's (*officinale*) herb appears to have been a comfrey of creamy-white flower. In the last century, however, plants with blue, purple and pure white flowers were imported from Russia and Turkey for pharmaceutical purposes, and to extract the plant's healing property known as *allantoin*. These newer strains have hybridised with the creamy-white flowered comfrey to give a range of pale colours.

Comfrey of any variety can be turned to good use in gardening as a fertiliser rich in potash. Mature leaves and stems are sometimes dug straight into the soil for this purpose. Alternatively, the leaves and stems can be collected into a plastic bag pierced with small holes, and then left plunged in a bucket of water. Once it has turned well brown and putrid, the water can be applied as a liquid to feed to tomatoes, vegetables or any other crop.

28

family: **daisy**

situation: **sun & semi-shade**

colour: **purple**

height: **30–60cm (12–35in)**

in flower: **June–September**

ground: **moderately fertile**

cultivation: **seed**

Common Knapweed

Centaurea nigra

Common Knapweed has the appearance of a thistle, but the leaves are roughly lanceolate, not prickly. A dark globular head beneath the purple brush of florets has given the plant more casual names: 'Hard-heads' and – disparagingly in Ruskin's *Proserpina* (1885) – the 'Black Knapweed'. In England and lowland Scotland, the plant is usually found in meadows and on roadside verges; in the South on soil that is heavy and wet.

The Knapweeds are a valuable food source for many insects and these, in turn, feed small birds. In the garden, seed of Common Knapweed can be sown directly onto the ground where it is to flower and covered lightly with soil; it would normally grow along with grasses and flowers of the summer meadow such as Goat's Beard, Lady's Bedstraw, Devil's Bit Scabious and Ox-eye Daisy.

Greater Knapweed is similar to the common variety, but with the addition of extended and almost trailing florets. The Cornflower is also a Knapweed which was nearly eradicated from farmland by the use of herbicides. Its head is small, giving prominence to an intense blue or magenta flower.

> Now I grow old and flowers are weeds,
> I think of days when weeds were flowers;
> When Jenny lived across the way,
> And shared with me her childhood hours.

This first stanza of *Jenny* by the 'super-tramp' poet, William Henry Davies (1871–1940) is a reminder that wild flowers were once the toys of country children, and their emblems of love and longing as they approached maturity and the time to marry. A girl would pluck the tops of Knapweeds as she thought of a boy she liked. If the head sprang new florets, this was a sure sign that he loved her. Imagination and superstition, woven into wild flowers, helped crystalise deep feelings. For those who gathered Knapweed, rather than be alone and emotionally paralysed, the flowers offered companionship and guidance.

family: **mallow**
situation: **sun**
colour: **pale mauve**
height: **30–90cm (12–47in)**
in flower: **June–September**
ground: **well-drained**
cultivation: **seed**

Common Mallow

Malva sylvestris

Although Tree Mallow (*Lavatera*) is in gardens everywhere, the beautiful Common Mallow sometimes tends to be forgotten. A wild perennial of verges and waste ground, the flower is pale mauve and clearly marked with deep purple lines running down the petals. These petals are so well tapered towards their base that the calyx can be seen in the gaps between them, like the rays of a green star.

In the centre of the flower a column of fused stamens holds aloft a pyramid of loose anther heads. Insects, guided by the petals' dark lines in the direction of the flower's honey-pits, are dusted with pollen. This is then carried onto other flowers of Mallow, a day older, and to where the stamens have collapsed to give way to dark-red feathery stigmas, receptive for the cross-fertilisation of the flower's seed.

Little 'fruits', which appear on the calyx after the flower has faded, are sometimes called 'pick cheeses' by children who enjoy their nutty flavour. Seed from these can be sown in spring or autumn, and lightly covered with soil, wherever new plants are to flower. Once the seedlings are up, they should be thinned out to 60cm (24in) apart. A variant of the flower with a more 'cottage garden' appearance is the wild Musk Mallow (*Malva moschata*). Although the lobes of its petals are 'torn', the upper leaves of this plant are nicely segmented; both flower and foliage are fragrant.

The discovery of Mallow pollen in Roman remains in northern Britain suggests it may have been imported from central Europe for medicinal purposes. Pliny the Elder (AD23–79), a collator of ancient wisdom, declared a daily 'spoonful of the mallows' to be preventative of all illnesses. A decoction of the leaves boiled in water was taken to calm fevers, and a lotion of the same was said to alleviate painful swellings. Mucilage of the roots, of the variety known as Marsh Mallow (*Althaea officinalis*), once provided a chewy filling in the delicious chocolate-coated biscuits of that name. Today it is somewhat rare in the wild and, as far as I know, only used in toiletries and cosmetics.

family: **daisy**

situation: **sun**

colour: **yellow & gold**

height: **20–50cm (8–20in)**

in flower: **June–September**

ground: **light, well-drained**

cultivation: **seed**

Corn Marigold

Chrysanthemum segetum

This intense yellow flower is one of the constituents of a cornfield flower-seed mixture (*see* p.36, Corn Poppy). Bought singly, however, Corn Marigold can either be mixed to one's own liking or grown in a clump next to other annuals or perennials. Although it seldom features now in the smaller wildflower manuals, Corn Marigold is too good to be overlooked as a garden plant: the several flower heads on each stem are accompanied by foliage that is slightly glaucous, and, as with all the chrysanthemums, the leaves are deeply notched. The seed needs to be sown thinly in spring where it is to flower – or in autumn if part of a mixture – then lightly raked into the soil. After flowering the plants can be left to reseed.

Remains of Corn Marigold have been excavated from archaeological sites of the Neolithic era, but not earlier. The weed probably came in with corn from southern Europe. Kings of England from Henry II (1133–1189) onwards enacted laws in a vain attempt to eradicate it. Court Rolls of the fourteenth century ordered tenants to uproot '*quondam herbam vocatam gold*' (a certain plant called 'Gold'). Farmers took to fields with teams of helpers to pull it up, or with the aid of long-handled forks attempted to hook out the nuisance from among the corn. The use of herbicides in the second half of the last century succeeded in clearing it out, where more than nine centuries of laborious effort had largely failed.

Where it still grows wild, in ancient fields on the coast of Cornwall, the Corn Marigold is now treasured. Elsewhere, it is being replanted where you might not expect it. Viewed from Old Rough Lane in Kirkby, on Merseyside, the open spaces between three high-rise flats on a June evening resemble a Monet painting, coloured by Corn Marigold, Ox-eye Daisy, Wild Poppy and Cornflower. At the edge of the field a group of lads chat up the girls. One of them sees me pick a single bloom of each flower and pretends disapproval. He has witnessed small children doing the same and is faintly amused. These fields have no supporting barley. The intention is that children on a city estate delight in dense masses of wild flowers that their ancestors once knew, play with them and think, perhaps to return home with some of these primary colours to keep alive in jars of water.

family: **poppy**
situation: **sun**
colour: **scarlet**
height: **20–60cm (8–24in)**
in flower: **June–August**
ground: **fertile, well-drained**
cultivation: **seed**

Corn Poppy

Papaver rhoeas

Corn Poppy was an unstoppable weed in fields of wheat and barley for more than four thousand years, until agricultural herbicides cleaned every crop. Nowadays we are made aware of the flower when it blooms on ground disturbed by motorway construction. Seeds dormant for up to 80 years are suddenly granted the conditions to germinate. The sight echoes the appearance of poppies on the shell-churned battlefields of the First World War, a scene which prompted the wearing of poppies on Remembrance Sunday:

Two other distinctive members of the poppy family: Welsh Poppy (*above*) and Horned Poppy (*right*). The Horned Poppy is abundant in less disturbed coastal regions. Similar in appearance, the Welsh Poppy favours rocky, shady areas.

... red poppies and a blue flower, great masses of them, stretched for miles and miles ... and the whole air up to a height of about forty feet, thick with white butterflies.
William Orpen (War artist at The Somme, 1917)
An Onlooker in France (1924)

Corn Poppy is gradually coming back to the countryside, mainly on set-aside land, although it is still scarce in the northwest of England and north Wales. In the old cornfields the flower nearly always appeared alongside Mayweed.

Today the National Wildflower Centre (*see* p.94) sells a seed mixture for derelict land, which contains Corn Poppy, along with eight other wildflower species. There are also packets of cornfield annuals which will create a flower bed of stunning colours: Corn Poppy with Corn Marigold, Cornflower and Corncockle. Once it is sown this seed requires no maintenance, except for watering during dry spells. At the end of the season 'allow the new seed to fall, cut back the dead foliage and rake the area well to leave over winter'.

Children have devised all manner of games with wild flowers: daisy chains, dandelion clocks and foxglove fingers. Using Corn Poppy, the trick is to fold down and tie the petals with a 'waistband' of fine grass. With its black hairy head exposed, the flower head is transformed, into a tiny doll.

family: **iris**
situation: **part-shade**
colour: **lavender**
height: **10cm (4in)**
in flower: **March, April**
ground: **well-drained**
cultivation: **bulb**

Crocus

Crocus tommasinianus

> Say, what impels, amidst surrounding snow,
> Congealed, the crocus' flamy bud to grow?
>
> *The Natural History of Selborne*, 1789

These lines from a hymn were quoted by Gilbert White to express his amazement that the spring crocus could flower 'by the beginning of March at the farthest, and often in very vigorous weather; and cannot be retarded but by some violence offered'. By violence he presumably meant decapitation. The tip of the sheath on the bud of a Spring Crocus – as with that of a Snowdrop – concentrates a metabolic warmth which can melt snow as it thrusts upwards, determined to bloom come what may.

Saffron was once the reason for cultivating crocuses of several varieties. This spice is now nearly always collected by harvesting the stigmas of just one variety, *Crocus sativus*, which needs to be grown in a hot climate. In medieval times, however, *Crocus vernus* was used in Europe for the production of saffron, and this was brought to Britain as the first type of spring crocus.

For centuries now, *C. vernus* has naturalised on several sites, especially in Nottinghamshire.

When plotted on a map these locations are seen to form a star-like pattern, with Lenton Priory at its centre. The botanist Steve Alton has suggested that the first consignment of these bulbs was imported by Benedictine monks, from fields around their mother-house at Cluny in Burgundy. Once established in Lenton's herbary at some time in the twelfth century, *C. vernus* then made its escape into nearby woods. Bulbs may also have been transplanted, by monks on 'perambulation' or by visitors to the priory gardens.

The dainty *Crocus tommasinianus* is another introduction which has since added to our stock of naturalised crocuses. In favourable conditions, the bulbs of this variety, perhaps more than any other, multiply rapidly, spreading a lavender carpet of flowers across lawns and into borders. Restricting them can be difficult and is, anyway, undesirable. Each flower is small and the leaves are fine; unlike bluebells and daffodils, their decomposition is not an eyesore. *C. tommasinianus* is widely available in garden centres and should be planted in partial shade. Its larger relative, *C. vernus*, is sometimes marketed as *C. purpureus*.

family: **willowherb**
situation: **sun**
colour: **lemon-yellow**
height: **80cm (31in)**
in flower: **June–September**
ground: **well-drained**
cultivation: **seed**

Evening Primrose

Oenothera glazoviana

The idea of a wild garden is placing plants of other countries, as hardy as our hardiest wild flowers, in places where they will flourish without care or cost.

William Robinson, *A Wild Garden,* 1903

Releasing hardy exotics into an unfenced wilderness is not an entirely novel proposal. Not at all uneasy about the possibility of unforeseen consequences, Robinson was a staunch advocate of the idea. His legacy is a mixed blessing: wild lupins are fine, provided they stay mainly on the sides of motorways – like the Michaelmas daisy on railway embankments – but on the hillsides of Wales and Scotland *Rhododendron ponticum* has run amok. Well aware that Japanese Knotweed is 'easier to plant than to get rid of', Robinson nonetheless proposed this indestructible thicket for 'copse or pondside'. The disaster is now plainly visible over much of our canal system.

One invasive foreigner which seldom earned disapproval is Evening Primrose, dramatically illustrated in a wood-block print (*A Wild Garden*, p.5) to underscore Robinson's recommend-ation. A North American import of the seventeenth century, the 'Long-leaved' variety has colonised roadsides, waste ground and sandy soil. Despite it not being native, Evening Primrose was given a wildflower imprimatur in the 1830s, in the form of a sonnet extolling its beauty by John Clare.

The plant is tall, not at all like a Primrose, with lemon-yellow long and cup-shaped flowers which, at evening, Clare described as 'almost as pale as moonbeams are'. Possibly too bright for the garden border, Evening Primrose is a flower for corners and edges: perhaps a sunny spot on the gravel of a driveway, where it can self-seed and be kept under control. The wild form growing on sand dunes, *Oenothera stricta*, has fragrance for a bonus.

Several non-wild varieties are more well known: *Oenothera biennis* is cultivated as a source of gamma linoleic acid (GLA), a valuable complementary medicine. And for the boundary of a rockery, the most popular is a perennial, a trailing and long-flowering Evening Primrose known as *Oenothera missouriensis*.

family: **figwort**

situation: **sun or shade**

colour: **mauve-purple**

height: **150cm (59in)**

in flower: **June–September**

ground: **dry**

cultivation: **seed**

Foxglove
Digitalis purpurea

Foxglove's mauve-purple bells are like the streamer of a falling rocket. They meet an upward spiral of leaves, becoming smaller as they go higher up the flower stalk. The lower leaves are the largest: fine-toothed at the edges, crinkly, coarse-veined on their upper surface and 'softly-downy' beneath. Each of the high-hanging flower tubes is beautifully mottled inside with crimson spots on a whitish background. The botanist John Hutchinson describes how an insect visiting the tube must clamber over white hairs which press it upwards against four arched anthers. The creature then emerges, dusted with pollen, to effect the fertilisation of stigma at its other ports of call.

Such a bright, tall spike of a flower is for growing beside walls and fences, beneath trees, in flower borders and in long grass. It can be moved and replanted without much ceremony and will happily tolerate drought and neglect. Seed germinated on open ground, in late spring or summer, produces plants to flower in the following year. The soil needs to be well drained but not sandy, and preferably somewhat acid. Once it has flowered and having cast copious amounts of seed, the plant dies.

'Foxglove' is such a strange name, and not derived from its location in woodland and bracken where foxes might conceal themselves. Children used to pick the flower tubes and slide them onto the tips of their fingers. The points which once attached the calyx to the plant-stalk were then imagined to be the claws of a fox's paw, useful for scaring people. It must be remembered however, that all parts of this plant are poisonous. As children cannot be relied upon not to suck their fingers or always to wash their hands, this game is not a good idea. Other names are 'Fairy gloves', 'Floppy dock' and 'Toad-tails'.

The plant's high toxicity did not prevent the use of Foxgloves as a herbal remedy, as a means of strengthening and slowing a feeble and palpitating heart-beat. Rather crude dosages often caused fatalities, stopping the heart altogether. In 1785 the physician, William Withering, in *An Account of the Foxglove*, argued for an accurate quantification of the leaf matter (*digitalis*) to make this medicine safe. His work marks the beginnings of modern pharmacology as a science of exact measurements.

family: **figwort**
situation: **sun or part-shade**
colour: **blue with white eye**
height: **up to 20cm (8in)**
in flower: **May–June**
ground: **all types**
cultivation: **plant**

Germander Speedwell

Veronica chamaedrys

The violet and cowslip, bluebell and rose are known to thousands – the Veronica is overlooked. The ploughboys know it, and the wayside children, the mowers, and those that linger in fields.

Richard Jefferies, *The Life of the Fields*, 1884

A plant of such allure ought never to be so unappreciated. When the poet John Keats (1795–1821) wrote that 'The trembling Eyebright showed her sapphire blue', he was referring to having at last seen Germander Speedwell, which at one time grew in abundance on the roadsides into London. Unfortunately, even before the march of bricks and mortar, it was picked to destruction for its dried leaves, an infusion of which makes a detoxicant tea.

Throughout Ireland, this flower was sewn into the coats of travellers, as the talisman of a safe journey, hence the name 'Speedwell'. In my home town of Liverpool, in the nineteenth century, Irish immigrants who had fled the potato famine extended their country lore to encompass the perils of the sea: they called all wild Veronica in the vicinity of the port, 'Sailor's Return'. The day may come when Germander Speedwell is emblazoned on a jet plane.

A species that is still common, Germander Speedwell is now a wild plant of grasslands and rough places throughout the country. The little flower's most curious feature are its two horn-like stamens which protrude from either side of the uppermost and largest petal. An approaching insect grasps these for support and, bending them, dusts its abdomen with pollen. Flying onto a younger flower – where the pollen is not yet discharged – it effects the desired cross-fertilisation. In prolonged, gloomy weather, the anthers hasten their maturity and the flower, closing up, fertilises itself.

Seed of Germander Speedwell is almost impossible to collect, but the plants are easily split up in spring and most gardeners who have it are usually happy to reduce their patch a little. A slightly shaded spot, in a lawn or hedgebank, is a good place to grow this attractive flower, provided it is not mown during the growing and flowering period in May.

family: **bellflower**

situation: **sun**

colour: **pale blue**

height: **25cm (10in)**

in flower: **July–September**

ground: **many types**

cultivation: **plant & seed**

Harebell

Campanula rotundiflora

This delicate and almost translucent blue flower hangs from a narrow stem which, when blown by the wind, causes the bell to leap upward. In the wild, the Harebell occupies a variety of nutrient-poor locations: including mountains, sand dunes, chalk meadows and acid heaths. The Northamptonshire nature-poet, John Clare, refers to the flower as the 'heathbell'.

Harebell seeds are usually sown in conjunction with the seeds of other flowers and grasses, to enrich the sward of a wildflower meadow. The fact that it is a fairly common countryside flower in no way detracts from its beauty. In the garden it can bring lightness, along with the foliage of fern-like perennials when, for example, it is planted between the hard edges of lichenous rock. In this situation, the round leaves (*rotundiflora*) at the base of the plant are hidden from view; what we see are the narrow upper leaves, complimenting the finely etched flower stem.

Another name for this plant, the Bluebells of Scotland, has sometimes caused it to be confused with the bluebells found in woodland (*see* p.20), which are rather a variety of wild hyacinth. The Harebell usually grows under open skies where it can enjoy full sun.

In Celtic folklore, Harebells are 'Fairies' thimbles' (Gaelic: *mearacan puca*; Manx: *mairanym ferish*), specifically those fairies at the service of witches, who were thought to have the power of transforming themselves into hares. Pennant-Melangell in Wales is one place where a Celtic legend of the hare's pacification has survived. This story, illustrated in carvings in the local church, assures local farmers that the fauna and flora of the valley no longer harbour pagan magic which might cause harm to sheep and cattle. It is hard to imagine that the name Harebell once conveyed deep suspicion of such a delightful flower, which in Welsh now has the name of *cloch yr eos*, bell of the nightingale.

family: **bedstraw**

situation: **sun or semi-shade**

colour: **greenish-yellow**

height: **15–100cm (6–39in)**

in flower: **July–August**

ground: **dry**

cultivation: **seed**

Lady's Bedstraw

Galium verum

The flowers of Lady's Bedstraw 'are beautifully arranged in little cymes, the whole forming an oblong mass of blossoms, each cluster having a whorl of small leafy bracts … slender stems are covered with minute reflexed hairs, which enable them to maintain their upright position amongst other herbage' (Hutchinson). To grow Lady's Bedstraw, seed should be sown in a tray in spring or autumn, lightly covered with soil and allowed up to twelve weeks to germinate. The seedlings should then be planted up in spring and spaced 50cm (20in) apart. This plant is ideal for growing with Harebell, Yarrow, Bird's-foot trefoil and the campions, and in a variety of locations including chalk banks and seaside gardens.

Well known to listeners to BBC Radio 4's *The Archers*, Lady's Bedstraw is the scriptwriter's favourite whenever a need arises to remind the audience that the parish of Ambridge is a flowery land. This particular bedstraw grows conveniently to hand in the wild on dry banks and grasslands – or hedgerows where the verge is grazed or cut short. It gained an early reputation from the first-century Greek author of *De Materia Medica*: Dioscorides recorded *galion* ('milk plant') as having the propensity to curdle milk. In the sixteenth century, the herbalist John Gerard in his *Herball* considered how Lady's Bedstraw was valuable to dairies, 'in Cheshire, especially about Namptwich where the best Cheese is made' (no prizes for guessing Gerard's birthplace). Since then, the art of using the plant as a rennet has sadly been lost.

The common name for the flower comes from an apochryphal Christian story, that 'Our Lady' gave birth to Jesus on a bed of bracken and white-flowered Galium. The bracken ignored the infant and lost its 'flower', while Galium witnessed the truth (*verum*) and was gifted flowers of gold. Like St John's Wort, Lady's Bedstraw was hung to sweet-savour places of prayer: 'It doth very well attemper the aire, coole and make fresh the place' (Gerard). The fragrance of the flower is honey and highly attractive to butterflies, the rest is full of coumarin, like the 'sweet vernal-grass' of meadows. Once they are dried, the thread-like leaves and stems for years retain the scent of newly mown hay.

family: **cabbage**
situation: **sun, part-shade**
colour: **purplish-white**
height: **15–40cm (6–16in)**
in flower: **April–June**
ground: **wetland**
cultivation: **seed, basal leaf**

Lady's Smock

Cardamine pratensis

Several plants have been called 'Cuckoo Flower' because they bloom about the time of the arrival of the cuckoo in spring. In respect of Lady's Smock, the coincidence which causes it to be known also by the bird's name is remarkable. A recent survey suggests that it begins to flower precisely in the twelve days before the first sound of a cuckoo, and not quite as John Gerard once stated: 'when the Cuckowe doth begin to sing her pleasant note without stammering' (*Herball*, 1597). Having made a point, however, Gerard himself chose the name Lady's Smock, which had come into use either because drifts of the flowers look silvery-white, like linen laid out to dry or the purplish-white frocks worn by milkmaids.

The flowers are very pale purple, with veins of a deeper purple, though they are prone to bleach in strong sunlight and can sometimes tend towards tones of lilac or pale pink. They attract all manner of insects: bees, flies, beetles, early-flying butterflies such as the Orange-Tip

and moths eager to probe the sepal-troughs and drink of the honey. Having been fertilised in the disturbance caused by some such visitor, the seed ripens to the point when, by a sudden splitting of its case, the contents are flung out to claim new ground for the plant.

Despite this and another efficient method of propagation from the leaves, Lady's Smock has noticeably declined in recent decades, due in part to improved drainage of pastureland. In the garden, seed of the flower 'should be planted in a patch of moist grass, or in a damp area near the pond'. Lady's Smock also enjoys a little shade, and would do well in wet ground near to trees, walls or fences. 'Plant with Ragged Robin for some early spring colour' (Stevens, 1987). The seed should be firmed into the wet soil in autumn. Another method of propagation is to pick a leaf from the base of a plant and place it onto moist seed compost in a tray. Like a begonia, Lady's Smock has the capacity to form roots from its basal leaves.

Marsh Marigold

Caltha palustris

The loss of flood meadows and their wild flowers has been a disaster for the beauty of the English countryside, matched only by the filling in over recent years of thousands of farm ponds and the loss of ancient flower-rich grasslands. Thoroughly drained farmland has caused the disappearance of many colonies of Marsh Marigold. In different parts of the country, 'King-cups', 'May-bubbles', 'Mollyblobs' and 'Yellow Crazies', are just a few of the local names for this luxuriant plant. The leaves are dark green and kidney-shaped. The flowers consist of five or six glossy golden petals opening from globular buds to form a cup (Greek: *kalathos*). The buds, preserved in vinegar, were once used like capers, not now recommended, as the plant is in fact somewhat poisonous. John Gerard's *Herball* (1597) commends it only for its beauty:

> great broad leaves somewhat round,
> smooth, of a gallant greene colour,
> slightly indented or purld about the edges:
> among which rise up thicke fat stalkes,
> likewise greene; whereupon doe grow
> goodly yellow floures, glittering like gold.

Through the pollen record, Marsh Marigold has been traced in aquatic sites dating from the end of the last glaciation. As enclosures regulated grazing, the plant was forced to the boundaries of the newly drained fields. For centuries it flourished in ponds and ditches. In 1594, the Shropshire poet Richard Banfield affectionately called it 'yellow boots – that grows by rivers and by shallow brooks'.

Marsh Marigold is easily grown in such boggy ground or beside a garden pond. If the edge of the pond liner has been tucked beneath and behind well-bedded perimeter stones, its roots and rhizome can be pushed into the mud trapped between these stones. For companion plants, there are Yellow Flag, Meadowsweet, Ragged Robin and Wild Angelica.

Old country inns often retained paddocks where travellers once penned and refreshed their horses. On these unimproved pastures wild flowers went unharmed. Consequently, in parts of Lancashire, Marsh Marigold is still referred to as 'Pubs' or 'Publicans', and Buttercup (*Ranunculus*), which is similar though somewhat smaller and often more numerous, is called 'Sinners'.

family: **geranium**
situation: **sun, part-shade**
colour: **violet-blue**
height: **30–80cm (12–31in)**
in flower: **June–August**
ground: **slightly chalk**
cultivation: **seed or plant**

Meadow Cranesbill

Geranium pratense

Cranesbills are wild geraniums, some of the most attractive flowers of the countryside. Seldom found these days across the breadth of fields, Meadow Cranesbill tends to grow on road verges and in field edges. It is a perennial with small and large leaves that are lobate and deeply segmented, in autumn tinged to a rich crimson. The best garden location is a spot allowed for the creation of a little wildflower meadow. Plants for this purpose can be bought from a specialist wildflower nursery or, alternatively, raised from seed. In the case of Meadow Cranesbill, the seeds need to be roughed up first between sheets of sandpaper in order to speed up their germination, then sown, each a few centimetres apart in open ground, and lightly covered with soil.

The flowers of Meadow Cranesbill are the largest of their kind (3cm). They bloom in succession and from a distance seem to merge into an 'azure film'. Each lasts a couple of days. On the first, the flower sheds pollen, on the second the style at its centre spreads a ray of five stigmas, ready to be fertilised. Insects, attracted by the flower's colour and honey, leave on the stigmas whatever pollen has attached to them from visiting flowers that have just opened.

The first-century Greek physician, Dioscorides, noted that the seed capsules of geraniums resemble the head and long bill of a crane, hence he called the plants by that bird's name – in Greek, *geranos*. The evocative shape is, in fact, a dispersal mechanism. When the seeds are ripe, a central axis grows from the flower stalk and lifts the 'bill' upwards. All five seed chambers are then put under such tension that when they break away at the base they coil upwards with a snapping sound. As the coil flies, the seed is catapulted to pastures new.

Such an amazing plant deserves honour. According to legend, the Prophet Mohammed (AD570–632), having laundered his shirt one day, spread it out to dry on a Mallow bush. Deeply sensitive to being so decorated, the Mallow blushed and, by the time the prophet returned, had transformed itself into the darker-flowered geranium.

(*Below*): Bloody Cranesbill is still to be seen on limestone in the Yorkshire and Derbyshire dales, despite having been preyed upon by unscrupulous gardeners.

family: **rose**
situation: **sun, part-shade**
colour: **greenish-cream**
height: **60–120cm (24–47in)**
in flower: **June–September**
ground: **moist**
cultivation: **seed or plant**

Meadowsweet

Filipendula ulmaria

'Decent weeds', is how the American writer Henry David Thoreau described Meadowsweet, and as 'unexhausted granaries which entertain the earliest birds'. Thoreau was charmed by the light and feathery flower clusters with their almond fragrance, and by the ferny leaves with an aroma like that of fruit and dill. Meadowsweet had been Queen Elizabeth I's favourite strewing-herb, recommended in Gerard's *Herball* (1597):

> The leaves and floures farre excel all other strowing herbes, for to decke up houses, to straw in chambers, halls, and banqueting houses in the summer time; for the smell thereof makes the heart merrie, [and] delighteth the senses.

Throughout Britain, Meadowsweet survives in ditches and on riverbanks. In the garden, its seed requires continuously moist soil if it is to germinate. Once established, plants can be divided in the autumn, growing to good effect alongside Purple Loosestrife, Yellow Loosestrife, Hemp Agrimony and Bugle. Earlier flowers for such boggy ground are Ragged Robin, Marsh Marigold and Lady's Smock.

The dainty coronals of Meadowsweet once inspired a grander title, 'Queen of the Meadows'. Each small flower is a ring of greenish-cream petals, within which stands a circlet of stamens, gold-tipped and crown-like, with what seems like an over-abundance of pollen. For instead of honey, which the flower lacks, the bees are offered an opportunity to make their 'bee-bread' from pollen sufficient to feed their nymphs and larvae. The plant, having been fertilised by the visitation of bees, subsequently grows seed-cases that look like stacks of tiny caterpillars, enticing birds to feast and scatter their contents.

The birds' feeding frenzy is what captured Thoreau's attention, as the flower tiers shone in stillness, or were tossed in the breeze to look like sea foam with a spume of flying petals. Mournful of a loss of wilderness – of wetlands drained, prairies greedily enclosed and forests utterly destroyed – he cursed progress: 'I should be glad, if all meadows of the earth were left in a wild state, if that were the consequence of men's beginning to redeem themselves.' (*Walden, or Life in the Woods*, 1854).

family: **primrose**
situation: **sun or shade**
colour: **sulphur yellow**
height: **8–15cm (3–6in)**
in flower: **March–June**
ground: **moist**
cultivation: **seed or plant**

Primrose
Primula vulgaris

Lovely the woods, waters, meadows,
    combes, vales,
All the air things wear that build this world
    of Wales.

In the Valley of the Elwy, 1877

The Elwy down to St Asaph is at the heart of the countryside that mattered most to Gerard Manley Hopkins, author of some of the most 'ecstatic' sonnets in the English language. The winding, lovely clear river is bounded on either side by narrow lanes, with banks brimming with wild flowers. The sulphur-coloured flowers of Primrose are in clumps everywhere, with Lesser Celandine and Stitchwort. 'Brilliancy, a sort of starriness', wrote Hopkins in his *Journal*, 'I have not the right word'. The Northamptonshire poet John Clare likewise laboured to do Primrose justice. He called them his 'timid beautys' in the poem *April Showers* (1832) and described how they cast a spell of happiness on the rain-cloud gloom of 'grey morn & swarthy eve'.

More so than the many-coloured, cultivated primulas, wild Primrose flowers are set on mounds of leaves that are oval, scalloped-edged, wrinkled on their upper surface and softly hairy beneath. The stems seem to unravel as they push upwards from the centre of each mound. The flowers on them are pale yellow, salver-like, with a 'brunny-eye' to guide an incoming bee.

Along with Cowslips (*top left*) and Oxlips (*bottom left*), Primrose, by an extraordinary twist of its evolution, has one of two types of flower; pin-eye or thrum-eye. The former have long-stalked pistils which hold the stigma at the mouth of the flower-tube, stamens are low down in the tube. In thrum-eyed flowers the pistil is short, the stigma low down, hidden by stamens at the top of the tube. This neat reversal means that a bee brushes the same areas of its body against different parts of the flowers, causing cross-pollination.

To grow wild Primrose, the seed should be pressed lightly onto the surface of the soil and kept damp over winter, covered with glass and partly shaded. In springtime the seedlings may then be transplanted. Once they are planted into a grassy bank, spare them the mower until the end of June. Hopefully they will reseed and extend along the bank.

Cowslips (*above*) were once common on pastureland before the use of chemical fertilisers. Oxlip (*below*) survives only in a few woodlands in southern and eastern England.

family: **lily**
situation: **semi-shade, shade**
colour: **white**
height: **30–35cm (12–14in)**
in flower: **April–May**
ground: **wet**
cultivation: **seed or bulb**

Ramsons (Wild Garlic)

Allium ursinum

Despite its acrid fragrance, Ramsons is one of the finest-looking of wild plants. The leaves are shiny, ovate, the texture of soft rubber. On a stem of triangular cross-section are produced pure white flowers in an inflorescence. They look particularly attractive on opening, as they spill from the bud. Provided the plant is controlled, confined to a small area, a drift of Ramsons can add a look of lush tropicality to an otherwise gloomy damp recess in a garden. It can be raised from either bulbs or seeds, sown straight onto the ground in autumn. When grown just for culinary purposes, this Wild Garlic has traditionally been used to flavour stews. As a garnish on sandwiches its tang is really quite mild, and certainly not as fierce as Wild Watercress.

Settlements in various parts of Britain gained a reputation for the pervasive smell of this pretty flower: Ramshope in Northumberland, Ramsbottom in Lancashire and Ramsholt in Suffolk, to name but three. The place-name, Ramsey, means 'an island of Ramsons'. The plant's name is derived from the Old English word *hrmsa*, which simply means 'wild garlic'. Richard Mabey, in *Flora Britannica* (1996), tells of how King Edmund, when granting land to Bishop Aelfric by the charter of AD944, defined the boundaries by reference to a Ramsons wood. There was no clearer landmark when maps were scarce and lacking accuracy.

In *The Names of Herbes* (1548), William Turner noted that 'this kind groweth also in gardines', which would suggest that Ramsons was transplanted from the wild mainly for use as medicine. The old West Country name, 'Brandy Bottles', confirms an observation made by a writer in the nineteenth century that the leaves of Ramsons infused in brandy were used in villages everywhere as a tonic.

family: **pink**

situation: **part-shade**

colour: **rose-pink**

height: **90cm (35in)**

in flower: **May–June**

ground: **moist (not wet)**

cultivation: **seed or plant**

Red Campion

Silene dioica

'Mother Dee' was once the formidable name that warned a child not to pick this flower. However, it was not the child's mother who died if this prohibition was ignored, but the flower itself, which soon expired. Almost immediately it is plucked, it shrivels and wilts. The now more life-affirming name, Campion, comes from the French word *champaign* (a field for horses), although the variety known as Red Campion generally does not grow on open fields, but in woodland and hedgebanks.

White-flowered Sea Campion (below) inhabits cliffs, shingle beaches and stable sand dunes.

Despite being somewhat straggly, Red Campion has always been a favourite for bringing colour to a shady border; the seed can be cast straight onto freshly raked soil. The flowers are a magnet for insects which, in turn, attract small birds. Other wild varieties – of white and pale pink campions – are called 'Catchfly'. These also draw into the garden many night-flying moths; expanding their petals to their fullest extent as darkness falls, they perfume the air with a clove-like fragrance.

A 1917 edition of Rankin's *A First Book of Wild Flowers* (see p.17) was proudly handed to me in Horwich Community Centre, Lancashire, by an elderly lady who had heard I was interested in wild flowers. On the inside cover, in neat child's handwriting, was the name and address of the original owner: 'E.L. Redfern, White Gates, Bowlacre Lane, Gee Cross'. I was assured the book had been treasured but not used since it was bought secondhand for 1s 6d. The pages were full of pressed flowers.

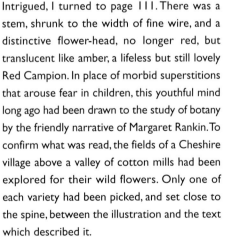

Intrigued, I turned to page 111. There was a stem, shrunk to the width of fine wire, and a distinctive flower-head, no longer red, but translucent like amber, a lifeless but still lovely Red Campion. In place of morbid superstitions that arouse fear in children, this youthful mind long ago had been drawn to the study of botany by the friendly narrative of Margaret Rankin. To confirm what was read, the fields of a Cheshire village above a valley of cotton mills had been explored for their wild flowers. Only one of each variety had been picked, and set close to the spine, between the illustration and the text which described it.

family: **dead-nettle**
situation: **sun, semi-shade**
colour: **purple-blue**
height: **10–30cm (4–12in)**
in flower: **June–October**
ground: **moist**
cultivation: **seed or plant**

Self-Heal

Prunella vulgaris

The last foxglove bells are nearly fallen ... and there is only one flower left to love among the grass, – the soft, warm-scented Brunelle ...

the most glowing of violets could not be lovelier than each fine purple gleam of its hooded blossoms ...

of all the flowers I know, this is the strangest.

John Ruskin, *Proserpina*, 1885

Self-Heal is a most desirable weed. Like clover, it is full of nectar for bees and butterflies and is no less important a flower for the lawn as buttercups, daisies and dandelions. The flower's 'spiky nap' is made up of tiers of little buds: each tiny flower appears at random, with two petals in the shape of lips, the upper arched like a hood and on the lower, three lobes. Visiting bees have to plunge into the flower, head first, and are obliged to back out, brushing pollen from their heads, having sucked the honey in a mere two seconds.

Self-Heal will not withstand doses of lawn 'weed and feed', but can grow flowers below the mower blades, provided these are set no lower than 10cm (4in). To establish it in grass, sow the seed onto bare patches, in spring or autumn, and sprinkle a little soil on top. Once established, the plants can be split in spring and allowed to spread again by means of their runners.

The High German name, 'Brunelle', from which the botanical Latin *Prunella* is derived, indicates the plant having been used to cure ulcerations of the mouth (*bräune*). In days when physicians seldom gave advice without payment, crushed leaves of Self-Heal were applied to a cut, a burn or a bruise, in the hope that the wound would heal itself. For its usefulness in this respect, it was probably carried by the early immigrants from Europe to North America, where it has settled at the expense of some of the native wild flowers. That it was a favourite in the New World is clear from the affectionate names given to it: 'Blue Curls' and 'Heart of the Earth'.

family: **lily**
situation: **sun**
colour: **chequered purple**
height: **20–40cm (8–16in)**
in flower: **March–May**
ground: **wetland**
cultivation: **bulb**

Snake's Head Fritillary

Fritillaria meleagris

Few people discover this plant in the wild. Most of us read about it first, or see pictures of the drooping reptilian flower heads on the packets of little bulbs sold in garden centres.

Snake's Head Fritillary once inhabited almost thirty counties. Now it is restricted to a similar number of protected sites, most of which are in the Thames Valley. There is a well-established population on the common land known as North Meadow, at Cricklade in Wiltshire. This is Lammas Land: closed to grazing on 13 February each year; the pasture is re-opened on old Lammas Day, 12 August, after the hay has been harvested. That long period of gestation allows the early summer flowers time to blossom and reseed themselves.

A few years ago a Snake's Head Fritillary flowered in a garden I know beside an ancient 'long-house' in Cheshire. No one there confessed to planting it, and there is no knowledge of a wild colony further north than Staffordshire, where records go back to 1787. Most botanists, however, suspect that the 'Checkered Daffodill', or 'Snake's Head Lily', as it was once called, has been around in parts of Britain since the end of the last Ice Age. Vita Sackville-West who, with her husband Sir Harold Nicolson, created the magnificent garden at Sissinghurst Castle in Kent, once described the enigmatic-looking flower as 'darkly glamorous, the snaky flower, scarfed in purple, like Egyptian girls'. When fully open, its lantern-like blooms are almost square, hence the term 'fritillary', meaning it is like a dice-box. *Meleagris* is Latin for a guinea-fowl, whose markings also resemble those on the petals. Quite often, in amongst the purple, there appears a white form with no chequerboard pattern (*left*).

Fritillaria meleagris is a very remarkable and arcane creature and deserves not just to be lost in the long grass. Plant the bulbs in a damp trough or some other suitably moist ground, where they can easily be seen and cause visitors to stop in their tracks.

The white-flowered form appears at random among the purple fritillaries.

family: **lily**

situation: **part-shade**

colour: **white**

height: **15–25cm (6–10in)**

in flower: **January–March**

ground: **rich, moist**

cultivation: **bulb**

Snowdrop
Galanthus nivalis

Few colonies of snowdrops have grown entirely from the wild, except in the West Country, which is perhaps why the feral flowers went unnoticed by botanists until late into the eighteenth century. The majority of places where they are now judged to be wild are usually the forgotten locations of cottages, or sites of ecclesiastical significance: churchyards and monasteries. There is a continuing tradition of decorating churches with snowdrops at Candlemas (2 February), the Feast of the Purification of Mary. This explains the old country names: 'February Fair Maid', 'Mary's Taper' and 'Dingle-dangle'. This last is not just a reference to the hanging flower head, but an association with the high-pitched mass bell. In the grounds of Thrumpton Hall, in the Trent Valley south of Nottingham, snowdrops grow in seemingly endless drifts, on land that was once part of a substantial Roman settlement. There is some speculation that the Romans may have introduced the flower.

Today, although they are not the first wild flowers of the New Year – that accolade goes to the less well-known Winter Aconite – Snowdrops are the flowers that many gardeners like to know are there, even if they are out of sight. I remember the elderly resident of a large house who could direct me to precisely the spot in an extensive and overgrown orchard where, hidden in the undergrowth, were clumps of Snowdrops that she and her husband had planted half a century before. She had not seen them for a decade, nor I guess had anyone else, but they were still growing there as if time did not exist.

Establishing snowdrops is not always an easy task. They tend to take to some gardens and not to others, usually favouring only moist, rich soil and some shade. The modern way of planting is to put the bulbs in the ground in autumn, but the old method is more reliable: plant the bulbs 3cm deep in spring, while they are 'in the green' – with leaves still attached.

Snowdrops growing at Wateredge Copse, Northchapel, Sussex.

family: **daisy**

situation: **sun**

colour: **pinkish-purple**

height: **up to 200cm (79in)**

in flower: **July–August**

ground: **moderately fertile**

cultivation: **seed**

Spear Thistle

Cirsium vulgare

No collection of wild flowers would be complete without a thistle. However, anyone who has had the misfortune to sit on a 'Picnic Thistle' (*Cirsium acaule*) will question the sanity of inviting its near relatives into the garden. That picnic-spoiler looks so innocently star-like and unobtrusively flat on otherwise downy-soft calcerous grassland.

Fortunately, there is a tall Melancholy Thistle (*Cirsium heterophyllum*) which is virtually unarmed. It has a lovely purple flower on a tall

stem and can be found on wet upland pasture, beside streams and in open woods. Thistles are ripe when the seed-heads start to open, allowing the seeds to be gently pulled out by their fluffy tails, and taken home for sowing into the flower bed. The Melancholy Thistle is so called because its flower bud droops while the stem is still growing.

The thistle first came to be an emblem for the Scots, by adoption from their French allies in the fourteenth century. As the English had taken the rose for a badge, in 1470 James III of Scotland stamped a thistle onto the silver groats in his coinage. This heraldic representation of the flower is most like the Spear Thistle, which can attain a height of almost 2 metres (78in). In the July ceremony known as 'Riding the Marches', such a specimen is paraded around the town of Langholm in Dumfriesshire, as a warning for lairds and upstarts not to meddle with the privileges of the people.

In the Midlands is a deliciously scented Musk Thistle (*Cirsium nutans*) which, in habit, appears to explode out of the ground. This is a variety that was painted by William 'Quaker' Pegg (1775–1851), one of the finest flower painters ever to paint onto Derby porcelain (*top left*).

(*Above*): Milk Thistle flower.
(*Above, top*): Dish decorated with Musk Thistle painting by 'Quaker Pegg', *c*.1800.
(*Right*): Exploding Thistle seedhead.

family: **carrot**

situation: **sun**

colour: **white**

height: **60–90cm (24–35in)**

in flower: **June–September**

ground: **moist**

cultivation: **seed or plant**

Sweet Cicely

Myrrhis odorata

This wild flower is native to the mountainous regions of South and Central Europe. Though scarce in the South of England, Sweet Cicely has naturalised in the UK from Derbyshire and Lincolnshire to the lowlands of Scotland, growing in many places – on roadsides, riverbanks and by woods, and in particular abundance in limestone areas. The flowers are nearly flat clusters carried on compound umbels which appear like windows of inverted triangles. Sweet Cicely is similar in appearance to Cow Parsley but with soft, ferny leaf-sprays from the lower stem.

Seed of this plant should be sown in autumn, the better for being on moist soil, and exposed to the cold of winter. By spring, the seedlings should be up, ready for thinning out before their tap roots take a hold. About this time, any older and well-established plants can withstand division and replanting.

The girl's name (in Greek, *seseli*) was used as early as the first century AD to identify this popular culinary herb. That it was sweet went without saying. The fresh leaves in a mixed salad counter any bitterness and with boiling fruit they remove the tartness. Almost the whole plant has the savour of aniseed; in France the leaves are dried and hung in closets to fragrance the stored linen.

In his sixteenth-century *Herball*, John Gerard speaks of Sweet Cicely as if it was the Elizabethan man's Viagra. He regularly boiled the roots and ate them steeped in French dressing, considering such food 'very good for old people that are dull and without courage … it increaseth their lust and strength'. Today, the seed cases are pickled and eaten as a delicacy, whilst in the North of England the same oily parts are used by wood-turners – rubbed onto newly cut hardwood they give it a fragrant sheen. The crushed seed of Sweet Cicely mixed with wax is a traditional recipe for furniture polish, although the seed has a different scent – it smells similar to cloves.

family: **violet**
situation: **semi-shade**
colour: **cobalt-blue, white**
height: **10–15cm (4–6in)**
in flower: **February–April**
ground: **rich, moist**
cultivation: **plant**

Sweet Violet

Viola odorata

Like Sweet Violet, the Hairy Violet (*above*) prefers calcerous soil. Dog Violets (*below*) will grow in almost every garden.

Shortly after Napoleon's death on the island of St. Helena, on 5 May 1821, a locket was found among his personal effects. Contained within it were petals of Sweet Violets, picked from the grave of his beloved Josephine. Of all flowers, the Empress of France had adored roses (*see Old Roses*, also in the *Gardens by Design* series), but no rose of that time bore her title. Instead, the petals of this common wild flower sufficed for remembrance of her.

A chemical composition known as ionine gives to the Sweet Violet what appears to be a fleeting scent. But it does not, in fact, lose its fragrance. Ionine has the capacity to dull a sense of smell. Leave Sweet Violets and come back to them and 'the perfume will return in fullness of strength, only to disappear again. It is this quality which has attributed so much to the charm of the violet for one can never become intoxicated with an excess of its sweet fragrance' (Genders, 1971).

Few flowers have received so much attention from poets: notably Herbert, Milton, Keats, Wordsworth, and Shakespeare, who mentions Sweet Violets on eighteen occasions. In the monastic herbaries, leaves of the plant were highly regarded as a medicine once recommended by the Greek physician, Hippocrates (5th–4th century BC). They are still in use as an antiseptic and in poultices, for relief from the discomfort of abscesses and swellings. Anthony Ascham's *Little Herbal* of 1525 prescribes them as a cure for insomnia:

> Seep this herb in water and at even, let him soak well his feet in the water to the ancles, and when he goeth to bed, bind this herb to the temples and he shall sleep well by the Grace of God.

Sweet Violets are distinguished from the scentless Dog Violet (*bottom left* and p.7) by their lighter green, much larger leaves, and no branching of their stems. The scented Violets are most often on grassy banks and the edges of woods in chalk districts. They will grow in moist, shady parts of the garden, where there is sunlight in early morning or late evening. Germination from seed is unpredictable, but Violets also spread by means of runners, which allow for their division and replanting in spring.

family: **thrift**

situation: **sun, semi-shade**

colour: **rose-pink, white**

height: **10–20cm (4–8in)**

in flower: **April–May**

ground: **moist**

cultivation: **plant & seed**

Thrift

Armeria maritima

I remember well the strange plant depicted on the back of a twelve-sided threepenny bit. Unfortunately its meaning was entirely lost to non-botanical children. We preferred to spend our pocket money, not save it. Nobody really knows how Thrift came to get its name. One theory is that the name is a reference to how the narrow, tightly packed leaves are designed to retain as much moisture as possible, as it clings to cliffs and dunes, exposed to the drying effect of sea breezes. As with the lewisias and some of the saxifrages, the starry flowers are grouped on dense, rounded flower heads, and held aloft by narrow, flexible stems. They present a pink cloud, highly attractive to butterflies.

Along with alpine plants, Thrift is ideal for sink gardens and small areas of ground which lack shelter. Also, for good effect, it can be planted as if already naturalised, as a carpet encroaching onto a path or between the gaps of pavements: it is aptly termed 'strand pink' (*strandnellick*) in Norway. The poet and critic Geoffrey Grigson tells of a day on Annet, in the Isles of Scilly – land surrounded by sea and smothered in Thrift – which he calls 'Sea Pink'. He describes a journey across the island 'as like a dream of walking on soft rubber which has squirted into

flower'. Although the Thrift has had little medicinal use, there was once a belief that this family of plants might be a cure for lead poisoning, hence their latin name *Plumbago*. Richard Mabey notes that Thrift has 'a taste for lead-rich soils and is often found growing on mining spoil'.

The Cumbrian name, 'Midsummer Fairmaid', conjures up more romantic locations – rocky fells and marshland edges. In Devon and Cornwall, Thrift, not content with shingle, has taken to growing on dry stone walls. Imagine the effect of wind whipping across a quilt of Thrift and the Gaelic name *tonn a chladarich* – the beach wave – makes perfect sense.

(*Below*): Sea Pink growing on Anglesey and (*below right*) Purple Thrift.

family: **borage**
situation: **sun**
colour: **purple-violet**
height: **80cm (31in)**
in flower: **June–September**
ground: **any well-drained**
cultivation: **seed**

Viper's Bugloss

Echium vulgare

Viper's Bugloss grows on dry, sandy and calcerous soils, even on builders' rubble, often in the company of Weld, a plant once cultivated for its yellow dye. If the garden soil is slightly acid, however, the seed should still germinate, provided it is sown in late summer and the seedlings thinned out to about 50cm (20in) apart. A rapidly developed tap-root, like that of a Dandelion, prevents the possibility of later transplanting.

Humming with bees, Viper's Bugloss is an awesome sight: sprays of purplish-violet flowers extruding red, tongue-like stamens, and 'fruits' like adders' heads. Those who believed in the ancient 'Doctrine of Signatures' saw in the plant one of the many examples of apparent mimicry, as if wild flowers were showing sympathy with the sufferings of sentient beings. So universal are these resemblances that signaturists believed that every ailment had a remedy, indicated somewhere in the appearance of a plant.

The Greek physician, Nicander, in a poem about venomous animals, had claimed that the viper plant (*echion*) succeeded as an antidote, when a viper (*echis*) bit the Athenian statesman Alcibiades (450–404BC) in his sleep. Medical opinion throughout Europe was consolidated in this view by the first-century Sicilian physician, Pedanius Dioscorides. He recommended 'this most gallant Herb of the Sun' as a prophylactic and panacea for snake bites. Other, more soundly based, claims followed: a decoction of the seeds was widely used to stimulate breast milk and an infusion of the basal leaves to revitalise the kidneys and ease lumbago. Viper's Bugloss proved a useful remedy, irrespective of unproven claims that it neutralised snake venom. I wonder if its use by monks, as a cure for the sin of sloth (*accidie*), gave rise to the notion that whoever took this medicine gained the strength and vitality of the 'tongue of an ox' (*bouglossos*)?

family: **lily**

situation: **sun, part-shade**

colour: **yellow**

height: **22–35cm (9–14in)**

in flower: **March–April**

ground: **moist**

cultivation: **bulb**

Wild Daffodil

Narcissus pseudonarcissus

They grew among the mossy stones about and about them; some rested their heads upon these stones as on a pillow for weariness; and the rest tossed and reeled and danced, and seemed as if they verily laughed with the wind, that blew upon them over the lake.

On 15 April 1802, Dorothy Wordsworth recorded the scene, in Growbarrow Park by Ullswater, that inspired her brother to write the poem, 'Daffodils', which contains the famous first line, 'I wandered lonely as a cloud...'

To see Wild Daffodils – in Cumbria; Farndale, Yorkshire; on the Sussex Weald; in South Devon; at Newent in Gloucestershire – makes one wonder why so many experts choose a different variety to naturalise in parks and woods. The yellow trumpet is long, the perianth petals pale, the leaves somewhat glaucous and, compared to most cultivated varieties, the stem is shorter. As Dorothy Wordsworth suggests, rather than stand to attention, the Wild Daffodil usually leans in some random direction. None of the cultivated relatives is so elegantly proportioned, although some of the white forms are near rivals for sheer beauty.

The Greek *asphodelus*, from which the common name is derived, was in mythology a white lily. Grown in the meadows of the underworld, the plant was the property of Persephone, queen of that country. A Roman version of this legend had Proserpina, as she had by then become, abducted in her sleep by the god Pluto. As his chariot sped heavenward, flowers from her wreathed crown fell to earth and turned yellow.

Writers of the sixteenth century regarded the arcane flower with great affection; they spoke of 'daffodowndillies' and rejoiced that it grew everywhere. Shakespeare, in *A Winter's Tale* (IV, iii), alluded to the Roman story and praised:

> ... daffodils,
> That come before the swallow dares, and take
> The winds of March with beauty.

Prior to the Second World War, Wild Daffodils were far too often accounted as weeds, to be dug up and destroyed, and this in part explains their scarcity. Our cultivated versions are no replacement for the originals. The weeds should be re-planted, in long grass, beneath trees, and spared the intrusion of the lawnmower until June.

family: **honeysuckle**
situation: **part-shade**
colour: **cream to purple-red**
height: **up to 6 metres (20ft)**
in flower: **June–September**
ground: **well-drained**
cultivation: **seed or plant**

Wild Honeysuckle

Lonicera periclymenum

Good Lord, how sweetly smells the honeysuckle
In the hush'd night, as if the world were one of utter peace, and love, and gentleness!

Alfred, Lord Tennyson
Idylls of the King, part 2 (1859)

Each new spray of Wild Honeysuckle is of creamy, long finger-like buds, curving upwards. With the onset of night individual buds straighten and, once they are horizontal they break into flower. First the slender under-lobe curls back upon itself, followed shortly after by the backward curving of the broad upper-lobe; stamens and style protrude as if shot from the flower tube. Glands on the tube's walls pour forth honey and a heady scent guides long-tongued hawk-moths, sometimes several hundred metres distant, towards the visible whiteness of the petal's inner surfaces.

For centuries, this extravagant flower of the woodlands has enchanted gardeners. Wherever a well-placed seat can catch the warmth of the setting sun, Wild Honeysuckle has been planted, to compensate the loss of daylight with the gain of a most powerful fragrance. The stem entwines (Greek: *perikleia*) whatever shrub, tree or trellis, it climbs, and so it was known as the Woodbine (William Turner's 'Woodbynde'). Shakespeare remarked on its seemingly gentle embrace, when in fact the grip is so tight that the luckless host is invariably imprinted, and sometimes charmingly distorted to the shape of a stick of barley sugar.

Seed of Wild Honeysuckle can be sown in autumn, though it may take a while to germinate. A ready-grown plant is easier and quicker, but be sure it is the native variety as most have the same somewhat glaucous leaves. For, as well as the creamy flowers, there are the luscious, translucent red berries for the birds, and raffia-like peeling bark on the ageing stem, providing material for the nests of dormice and birds.

family: **buttercup**
situation: **part-shade**
colour: **white**
height: **15cm (6in)**
in flower: **March–April**
ground: **moist**
cultivation: **rhizome**

Wood Anemone

Anemone nemerosa

The Greek word *anemone* means 'daughter of the wind', hence Wood Anemone is sometimes called the 'Windflower'; in France, *les herbes au vent*. In a March gale the star-like flowers appear to be wildly dancing. To prepare the ground for their planting, make sure the soil is loose with lots of leaf-mould, and tuck in the rhizomes 20cm (8in) apart. To come across Wood Anemone in the wild invariably indicates a site that has long been undisturbed: the seed in Britain is usually infertile and, in order to propagate, the plants must extend their rhizomes, their 'tuberous roots'. This expansion proceeds at the stately pace of a metre every hundred years.

The expansion of Wood Anenome to a cluster of flowers may take several years.

Taking advantage of the light, Wood Anemone breaks into flower before trees are in leaf. Each flower has six sepals – white, sometimes blush-pink underneath – held aloft on wiry looking stems. The leaves below consist of three leaflets, intricately cut and notched. On a still day swathes of the plants have a lovely musk fragrance.

The Wood Anemone was a favourite of the talented Irish-born horticulturist William Robinson. He planted it in his re-creations of wild woodland and in rock outcrops, stone laid on soil to give the appearance of natural strata. He outlived his famous admirer, the garden designer Gertrude Jekyll. When she died in 1932, Robinson, almost paralysed and in his nineties, struggled to attend her funeral. The two had held each other in high regard, and in 1899 Robinson had handed over to her the editorship of *The Garden* magazine, which he had founded.

Robinson's own career as a garden designer had been somewhat blighted in his youth, by a quarrel with the owner of the estate at Ballykilcaven in County Laois. It was rumoured that he had quit his job there on the night of a severe frost, leaving the doors and windows of the hothouses open, the fires out, causing a massacre of his employer's collection of exotics. It was no secret that Robinson abhorred artificiality in gardening. He would sooner plant hosts of Wild Anemones than a single flower reared in a hothouse. He loved the excitement of wind and weather, hence his love of the 'Windflower'.

family: **wood sorrel**

situation: **shade, part-shade**

colour: **white**

height: **5–10cm (2–4in)**

in flower: **April–May**

ground: **any**

cultivation: **seed or plant**

Wood Sorrel

Oxalis acetosella

This small plant is often rampant in the dark corners of gardens and backyards. Tolerant of dry conditions, Wood Sorrel is sometimes the only wild flower that will grow beneath a very shady tree, or work its way along the crevices around yard tiles and paving. The seed germinates easily, provided there is no competition from other small plants and grasses. In normal shade, the clover-like leaves of Wood Sorrel lie fully open. Reacting to stormy weather, direct sunlight or the onset of night, the leaves fold onto their stem to form a pyramid. One need only touch the leaves, or drop a hat over the plant, to stimulate this protective response.

The flowers of Wood Sorrel are a translucent white. On their fading, the flower stem curves downward into the leaves for protection. Once the seed is ripened amid the leaves, the stem straightens once more to gain height: a powerful tension in the seed against the inelasticity of its own outer membrane then causes such a violent splitting of this coat that the ripe seed is propelled several metres from the plant. A light vibration of the stem will often trigger the working of this spectacular 'sling-fruit' mechanism.

Infusions of Wood Sorrel were at one time prescribed as a gargle to cure mouth ulcers, and used externally to treat scabies. The whole plant is so rich in oxalic acid that it is a potent but somewhat dangerous source of medicine. More than a mild dose will cause poisoning. Since Victorian times, botanists have inclined to the opinion that Wood Sorrel and not Clover was the original Irish Shamrock. The appearance of its five-petalled flower at Eastertime was taken as a reminder of the five wounds of Christ, giving it yet another name, the 'Alleluia'. When St Patrick (c.398–c.461) preached the Holy Trinity, he is thought to have used the trifoliate leaves of Wood Sorrel as his visual aid. Thereafter the plant became a sign of 'mysticism and truths too deep for mortal comprehension'.

family: **iris**
situation: **prefers sun**
colour: **yellow, dark-veined**
height: **40–150cm (16–60in)**
in flower: **May–July**
ground: **wetland**
cultivation: **seed or rhizome**

Yellow Flag

Iris pseudacorus

Had this been but a Himalayan rarity, with what glory, snobs that we are, would we not have displayed it, bright in the garden to envious visitors.

Robert Gathorne-Hardy,
Wildflowers in Britain (1938)

Yellow Flag used to be thought of as too common for a pretty garden, but intensive agriculture has put paid to this disdain. The loss of farm ponds, flood meadows and rivers that meander, has chased wild iris from many of its old haunts, turning the flower into something of a rarity in some places. It is now undergoing a revival, on the edge of garden ponds.

Fortunately, Yellow Flag is robust and flourishes in the countryside still, in neglected water-courses, in unscoured ditches and on the squelchy margins of protected lakes and waterways. As in the wild, so in a garden, the rhizomes require only mud in which to put down their roots. The leaves sprout from their watery underworld like numerous Excaliburs, henching round a flower which has an extraordinary combination of recurved long, and erect short petals. This elaborate shape, once adopted by Louis VII as an heraldic device, became the emblem of medieval France, the *Fleur-de-lis*, the flower of Louis.

In Japan, wild iris is a favourite on colourful embroidery, and in Buddhist lands generally this flower is seen as nature's prayer-flag, a sign of peace and joyfulness. Indeed, it is hard to watch Yellow Flag and water, animated by the wind, and feel anything other than tranquillity and pure happiness.

Wild Flowers on National Trust Land

The following Trust properties either grow native flowers in their gardens or have an abundance of them in the wild in adjacent parkland, woods and fields. This list is by no means comprehensive and more information is to be found in the NT and National Trust for Scotland handbooks.

Acorn Bank, Temple Sowerby, nr Penrith, Cumbria Tel. 017683 61467

Anglesey Abbey, Lode, Cambridgeshire Tel. 01223 811 200

Antony, Torpoint, Plymouth, Cornwall Tel. 01752 812 191

The Argory, 144 Derrycaw Road, Moy, Co. Armagh, NI Tel. 028 8778 4753

Arlington Court, nr Barnstaple, Devon Tel. 01271 850 296

Attingham Park, Shrewsbury, Shropshire Tel. 01743 708 123

Baddesley Clinton, nr Warwick Tel. 01564 783 294

Bodnant Garden, Conwy, Cymru Tel. 01492 650 460

Brodick Castle (NTS), Isle of Arran Tel. 01770 302462

Castle Fraser (NTS), Sauchen, nr Aberdeen Tel. 01330 844651

Chirk Castle, Wrexham, Cymru Tel. 01691 777 701

Cliveden, Taplow, Buckinghamshire Tel. 01494 755 562

Crathes Castle (NTS), Banchory, nr Aberdeen Tel. 01330 844651

Culzean (NTS), Maybole, South of Ayr Tel. 01655 884400

Drum Castle (NTS), Peterculter, nr Aberdeen Tel. 01330 844651

Emmetts Garden, Ide Hill, Sevenoaks, Kent Tel. 01732 751 509

Erddig, Wrexham, Cymru Tel. 01978 315 151

Farnborough Hall, Banbury, Warwickshire Tel. 01295 690 002

Florence Court, Enniskillen, Co. Fermanagh, NI Tel. 028 6634 8249

Glendurgan Garden, nr Falmouth, Cornwall Tel. 01326 250 906

Killerton, nr Exeter, Devon Tel. 01392 881 418

Kingston Lacy, Wimborne Minster, Dorset Tel. 01202 880 413

Lacock Abbey, nr Chippenham, Wiltshire Tel. 01249 730 227

Leith Hill, Coldharbour, Surrey Tel. 01306 711 777

Lyme Park, Disley, Cheshire Tel. 01663 766 492

Newhailes (NTS), Musselburgh, Edinburgh Tel. 0131 653 5599

Nymans Garden, Haywards Heath, W. Sussex Tel. 01444 400 321

Penrhyn Castle, Bangor, Gwynedd, Cymru Tel. 01248 371 337

Petworth Park, W. Sussex Tel. 01798 343 929

Plas Newydd, Anglesey, Cymru Tel. 01248 715 272

Plas yn Rhiw, Llyn Peninsula, Cymru Tel. 01758 780 219

Polesden Lacey, nr Dorking, Surrey Tel. 01372 458 203

Powis Castle, Welshpool, Powys, Cymru Tel. 01938 551 944

Rievaulx Terrace & Temples, Helmsley, N. Yorkshire Tel. 01439 798 340

Rowallane Garden, Sainfield, Co. Down, NI Tel. 028 9751 0131

Saltram, Plymouth, Devon Tel. 01752 333 500

Scotney Castle Garden, Lamberhurst, nr Tunbridge Wells, Kent Tel. 01892 891 081

Sheffield Park Garden, Sheffield Park, E. Sussex Tel. 01825 790 231

Sizergh Castle, nr Kendal, Cumbria Tel. 015395 60070

Standen, East Grinstead, W. Sussex Tel. 01342 323 029

Stourhead, nr Warminster, Wiltshire Tel. 01747 842 030

Studley Royal & Fountains Abbey, Ripon, N. Yorkshire Tel. 01765 643 197

Uppark, S. Harting, nr Petersfield, W. Sussex Tel. 01730 825 857

The Weir, Swainshill, nr Hereford Tel. 01981 590 509

Wimpole Hall, Arrington, nr Cambridge Tel. 01223 207 257

Winkworth Arboretum, nr Godalming, Surrey Tel. 01483 208 477

The National Trust also owns farms, woods, fells, heaths and commons rich in wild flowers: more than a quarter of the Lake District National Park, several beautiful dales in Yorkshire and Derbyshire and botanically valuable sites in the south of England at Devil's Dyke, Harting Common, Selborne Hill and Common, and in the West Country, Melbury Down and Studland Heath. Ancient woodlands are among the Trust's best wildflower properties in the Midlands, and in East Anglia there are preserved wetland sites such as Wicken Fen and Horsey Mere. Around the coast, areas of importance to wildlife in general include St Aiden's Dunes in the north-east, Formby Sand Dunes on the coast of Lancashire, the many unspoilt beaches and marshes of the Suffolk and Norfolk coast and flower-rich coastal cliffs in Dorset, Devon and Cornwall.

In north Wales, the Trust owns large areas of land in Snowdonia National Park, including Cwm Idwal Nature Reserve and the Dolmelynllyn Estate near the Mawddach Estuary. In south Wales, flower-abundant fields and cliff-tops along the route of the Pembrokeshire Coastal Path have been acquired for conservation by the National Trust. Scenic areas of the coast of Northern Ireland are also in the Trust's care and inland the Murlough Nature Reserve, the foreshore of Strangford Lough and the Crom Estate on Lough Erne.

The National Trust for Scotland owns large areas of upland: Mar Lodge in the Cairngorms, Ben Lawyers in the Central Highlands and Glencoe in Argyll – all rich in native flora – as well as several outstandingly beautiful wildlife areas in Ross-shire. Among the islands owned and protected by the NTS are Iona, Canna, St Kilda and Fair Isle.

THE NATIONAL TRUST
P.O. Box 39, Warrington, WA5 7WD
Tel. 0870 458 4000
enquiries@thenationaltrust.org.uk
www.nationaltrust.org.uk

THE NATIONAL TRUST FOR SCOTLAND
Wemyss House, 28 Charlotte Square,
Edinburgh, EH2 4ET
Tel. 0131 243 9343
development@nts.org.uk www.nts.org.uk

Other Wildflower Organisations

BOTANICAL SOCIETY OF THE BRITISH ISLES
The Natural History Museum,
Cromwell Road, London, SW7 5BD
Tel. 020 7942 5000
www.BSBI.org.uk

BRITISH ECOLOGICAL SOCIETY
26 Blades Court, Deodar Road, Putney,
London, SW15 2NU Tel. 020 8871 9797
info@britishecologicalsociety.org
www.britishecologicalsociety.org

COMMON GROUND
'Local Community Traditions in Respect of Nature'
21 High Street, Shaftesbury, SP7 8JE
Tel. 01747 850820
info@commonground.org.uk
www.england-in-particular.info

COUNTRYSIDE COUNCIL FOR WALES
'Sites of Special Scientific Interest and National Nature Reserves'
Maes-y-Ffynon, Penrhosgarnedd, Bangor,
Gwynedd, Cymru, LL57 2DW
Tel. 0845 130 6229
enquiries@ccw.gov.uk
www.ccw.gov.uk

ENGLISH NATURE
'4,000 Sites of Special Scientific Interest and National Nature Reserves'
Northminster House,
Peterborough, PE1 1UA
Tel. 01733 455100
enquiries@english-nature.org.uk
www.english-nature.org.uk

FLORALOCALE
'Promotes Use of Native Origin Seeds and Plants'
Denford Manor, Hungerford, RG17 0UN
Tel. 01488 689035
info@floralocale.org
www.floralocale.org

LANDLIFE & THE NATIONAL WILDFLOWER CENTRE
'To Create Wildflower Habitats and Raise Awareness in Urban Areas'
Court Hey Park, Liverpool, L16 3NA
Tel: 0151 737 1819
info@landlife.org.uk
www.nwc.org.uk
www.landlife.org.uk
www.wildflower.org.uk

NATIONAL PARKS AUTHORITY
126 Bute Street, Cardiff, CF10 5LE
Tel. 029 2049 9966
enquiries@anpa.gov.uk
www.anpa.gov.uk

PLANTLIFE
'Campaigns to Save Wildflower Habitats'
14, Rollestone Street, Salisbury, SP1 1DX
Tel. 01722 342 730
enquiries@plantlife.org.uk
www.plantlife.org.uk

SCOTTISH NATURAL HERITAGE
'Sites of Special Scientific Interest and National Nature Reserves'
12 Hope Terrace, Edinburgh, EH9 2AS
Tel. 0131 446 2277
www.snh.org.uk

WILDFLOWER SOCIETY
'Conservation and Education'
82A High Street, Sawston,
Cambridge, CB2 4HJ
www.rbge.org.uk/data/wfsoc

WILDLIFE TRUSTS
'Co-ordinates Care of 2,300 Nature Reserves'
The Kiln, Waterside, Mather Road,
Newark, NG24 1WT
Tel. 0870 036 7711
info@wildlife-trusts.cix.co.uk
www.wildlifetrusts.org

Specialist Suppliers

British Wildflower Plants
Burlingham Gardens, 31 Main Road, nr Burlingham,
Norfolk NR13 4TA
Tel. & Fax 01603 716615
linda@wildflowers.co.uk
www.wildflowers.co.uk

Chiltern Seeds
Bortree Stile, Ulverston, Cumbria, LA12 7PB
Tel. 01229 581 137   Fax 01229 584 549

Emorsgate Seeds
Limes Farm, Tilney All Saints, Kings Lynn,
Norfolk PE34 4RT
Tel. 01553 829 028   Fax 01553 829 803
wildseed@talk21.com
www.wildseeds.co.uk
Also at: Manor Farm, Langridge, Bath, BA1 8AJ
Tel. 01225 858 656

Flower Farms
Carvers Hill Farm, Shalbourne, Marlborough,
Wiltshire SN8 3PS
Tel. & Fax 01672 870 782
bobanderson@wildflowerfarms.com

Landlife Wildflowers Ltd, National Wildflower Centre,
Court Hey Park, Liverpool L16 3NA
Tel. 0151 737 1819   Fax 0151 737 1820
info@wildflower.org.uk
www.wildflower.org.uk

MAS
4 Pinhills, Wenhill Heights, Calne, Wiltshire SN11 0SA
Tel. & Fax 01249 819 013
shop@meadowmania.co.uk
www.meadowmania.co.uk

Naturescape
Lapwing Meadows, Coach Gap Lane, Langar,
Nottinghamshire NG13 9HP
Tel. 01949 860 592   Fax 01949 869 047
sales@naturescape.co.uk
www.naturescape.co.uk

Wild & Species Roses: Acton Beauchamp Roses,
nr Worcester, WR6 5AE
Tel. 01531 640 433   Fax 01531 640 802
www.actonbeaurose.co.uk

YSJ Seeds
Kingsfield Conservation Nursery, Broadenham Lane,
Winsham, Chard, Somerset TA20 4JF
Tel. & Fax 01460 30070
ysjseeds@aol.com

Select Bibliography

ABBOT, Hyacinth & HUTCHINSON, John, *A Bouquet of Wild Flowers*, Bruce & Gawthorn (undated)

AKEROYD, John, *The Encyclopedia of Wild Flowers*, Parragon (2002)

ANDREWS, Jonathan, *The Country Diary Book of Creating a Wild Flower Garden*, Henry Holt & Co. (1986)

ATASOY, Nurhan & RABY, Julian, *Iznik, the Pottery of Ottoman Turkey*, Alexandra Press (1989)

BAINES, Chris, *How to make a Wildlife Garden*, Elm Tree (1985)

BEARDSHAW, Chris, *The Natural Gardener, Lessons from the Landscape*, BBC Books (2003)

BENNETT, Jackie, *Wild about the Garden*, Boxtree (1998)

CARSON, Rachel, *Silent Spring* (1962), Penguin Classics (2000)

CLARE, John, *The Midsummer Cushion* (1834), Carcanet (1990)

COATES, Alice, *Flowers and their Histories*, Hulton Press (1956)

CORKE, H. Essenhigh & NUTTALL, G. Clarke, *Wild Flowers as they Grow*, Cassell (1911)

CULPEPER, Nicholas, *The Complete Herbal* (1649), Edited by David Potterton, W. Foulsham & Co. (1983)

DAVIES, W. H., *Collected Poems*, Jonathan Cape (1940)

DIOSCORIDES, Pedanius, *De Materia Medica* (English translation), 1934

GATHORNE-HARDY, Robert, *Wildflowers in Britain*, Batsford (1948)

GENDERS, Roy, *The Scented Wild Flowers of Britain*, Collins (1971)

GERARD, John, *The Herball* (1597), 2nd Edition enlarged and amended by Thomas Johnson, Adam Islip, Joice Norton & Richard Whitakers (1633)

GRAHAME, Kenneth, *The Wind in the Willows* (1908)

GRIGSON, Geoffrey, *The Englishman's Flora*, Phoenix House (1958)

HANKS, David, *The Decorative Designs of Frank Lloyd Wright*, Studio Vista (1979)

HOPKINS, Gerard Manley, *The Journals and Papers of Gerard Manley Hopkins*, OUP (1959)

HOPKINS, Gerard Manley, *The Poems of Gerard Manley Hopkins*, OUP (1967)

JEFFERIES, Richard, *The Life of the Fields*, Chatto & Windus (1884)

JEFFERSON-BROWN, Michael, *Wild Flower Gardening*, RHS (1990)

KEBLE MARTIN, W., *The Concise British Flora*, Rainbird (1965)

KIRKWOOD, Ralph & FOULDS, Margaret, *Plant Life in Ayrshire*, AANHS (1992)

MABEY, Richard, *Flora Britannica*, Chatto & Windus (1996)

MCMURTRIE, Mary, *Scots Roses*, Garden Art Press (1998)

ORPEN, William, *An Onlooker in France*, 1921, Parkgate (1996)

PHILLIPS, Roger, *Wild Flowers of Britain*, Pan Books (1977)

PLINY THE ELDER, *Natural History* (English translation), Penguin Classics (2003)

RANKIN, Margaret M., *A First Book of Wild Flowers*, Andrew Melrose (1909)

Legal Protection of Wild Flowers

ROBINSON, William, *The Wild Garden* (5th Edition) 1903, Century (1983)

ROBINSON, William, *The English Flower Garden* (1883), John Murray (1956)

ROTHSCHILD, Miriam & FARRELL, Clive, *The Butterfly Gardener*, Michael Joseph (1983)

RUSKIN, John, *Proserpina*, G. Allen (1874–1886)

SHEAIL, John, *Seventy-five Years in Ecology: The British Ecological Society*, BES (1987)

SOWERBY, John E. & JOHNSON, C. Pierpoint, *A Concise Encyclopedia of Wild Flowers* (1860), Wordsworth Editions (1989)

STEVENS, John, *The National Trust Book of Wild Flower Gardening*, Dorling Kindersley (1987)

TENNYSON, Alfred, Lord, *Idylls of the King* (1859), Penguin (1983)

THEOPHRASTUS, *Enquiry into Plants*, Heinemann (1916)

THOREAU, Henry David, *Walden, or Life in the Woods* (1854), Princeton University Press (1971)

TURNER, William, *The Names of Herbes* (1548), Ray Society (1965)

WALTON, Izaak, *The Compleat Angler*, Oxford World's Classics (1653)

WHITE, Gilbert, *The Natural History of Selborne* (1789), Penguin Classics (2003)

WILSON, Phil & KING, Miles, *Arable Plants – A Field Guide*, English Nature (2003)

WORDSWORTH, Dorothy, *Journals of*, Macmillan (1941)

All wild plants in Britain have some degree of legal protection. It is unlawful to dig out or uproot any of them without permission of the landowner. On Nature Reserves, Sites of Special Scientific Interest, National Trust and Ministry of Defence land the public is also prohibited from picking wild flowers unless by consent of the appropriate conservation agency.

Rare and endangered plants are listed in Schedule 8 of the 1981 Wildlife and Countryside Act. This makes it an offence for them to be picked, removed, traded or destroyed except by licence. It is also illegal to introduce into the wild, plants in Schedule 9 that may pose a threat to the native flora. Voluntary societies currently do not offer lists of the plants covered by the Schedules, but the Wildlife and Countryside Act and Wildlife (Northern Ireland) Order may be obtained from HMSO stationers. Schedule 8 is also on the internet: www.naturenet.net/law/sched8.html

When picking wild flowers for enjoyment, from such as a roadside verge or a footpath, collect just enough for personal use and avoid species that wilt too quickly. The blooms and any foliage should be taken from a large patch where the loss will not be noticed. Take care not to uproot whole plants. When photographing wild flowers, be careful not to crush seedlings, mosses and lichens in the undergrowth.

Acknowledgements & Picture Credits

My thanks go to Brenda Catherall for her assistance with research and Candida Boyes for reading the early drafts, also Paul and Sandra Christy, Richard Scott at the National Wildflower Centre and Charles Flower for their helpful advice. Louise McVey checked website information for me and Isabelle O'Reilly typed the text. Librarians at Liverpool Central Library and Oliver Hilliam of the CPRE Library have been exceptionally generous with their time.

In several parts of this book I have drawn on Richard Mabey's *Flora Britannica* for inspiration, particularly so for material about Corn Poppy, Snowdrop, Spear Thistle and Wild Daffodil. The unabridged version of Mabey's work is indispensable to anyone who has an interest in wild flowers as cultural phenomena; his book richly deserves the clutch of literary prizes it has won since publication.

Finally, I thank Barbara Mercer for her careful selection of the photographs and the design, also Fiona Screen and Margaret Willes at the National Trust, for their patience and encouragement.